Contents

Part 1: body systems

Part 2: control systems

Part 3: animal senses

Part 4: sensory adaptations

Contents

Part 1: body systems answers

Part 2: control systems answers

Part 3: animal senses answers

Part 4: sensory adaptations answers

1a: The circulatory system

Learning outcomes:

* Describe the double circulatory system;
* Identify the main structures in the mammalian heart;
* Describe how the cardiac cycle is coordinated;
* Explain the role of the SAN, AVN, Bundle of His & Purkinje fibres in the control of the cardiac cycle;

Fill in the gaps below to describe how a double circulatory system works.

The double circulatory system

The **m**_____ heart is described as a **d**_____ circulatory system because the heart has two separated halves. The left side pumps **o**_____ blood and the right side **d**_____ blood.

The left side of the heart pumps blood from the heart to various **t**_____ and **o**_____ in the body (**systemic** circulation) and the smaller, right hand side of the heart pumps blood to the **l**_____ (**pulmonary** circulation).

Match the groups of animals with the correct circulatory system.

Amphibians & reptiles   Closed, double system with a 4 chambered heart.

Birds & mammals   Often have an open system, great variation in heart structure.

Fish   Have a closed, double system with a 3 chambered heart.

Invertebrates   Closed, single system with a 2 chambered heart.

Draw a simple diagram of the heart with 4 chambers to show double circulation.

The circulatory systems consists of the veins, arteries & capillaries.

Animals such as and have a x2 system.

This means blood travels more efficiently round the body, transporting more O_2 & to the body cells.

The mammalian consists of chambers.

Some animals like have a   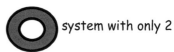 system with only 2 chambers.

Draw 2 simple diagrams to show how a single & double circulatory system work.

1a: The circulatory system

Learning outcomes:

* Describe the double circulatory system;
* **Identify the main structures in the mammalian heart;**
* Describe how the cardiac cycle is coordinated;
* Explain the role of the SAN, AVN, Bundle of His & Purkinje fibres in the control of the cardiac cycle;

Label the parts of the heart.

Answers:
1a=superior vena cava 1b=inferior vena cava 2=aorta
3=pulmonary artery 4=right atrium 5=pulmonary vein
6=right ventricle 7=left ventricle 8=left atrium
9=tricuspid valve 10=bicuspid/mitral valve
11=papillary muscles 12=chordae tendineae
13=semi-lunar valve (pulmonary) 14=septum

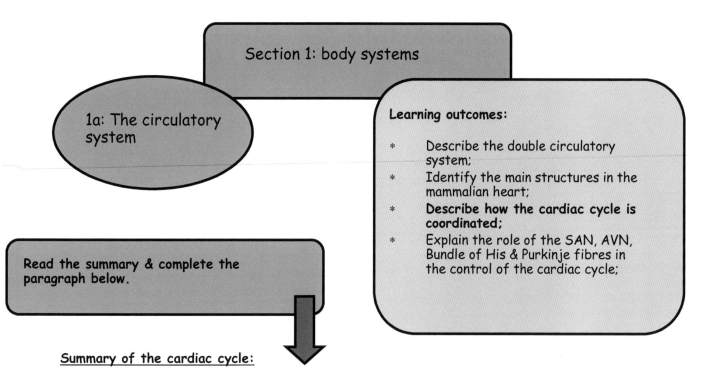

1a: The circulatory system

Learning outcomes:

*   Describe the double circulatory system;
*   Identify the main structures in the mammalian heart;
*   **Describe how the cardiac cycle is coordinated;**
*   Explain the role of the SAN, AVN, Bundle of His & Purkinje fibres in the control of the cardiac cycle;

Read the summary & complete the paragraph below.

Summary of the cardiac cycle:

1. *Diastole* – Atria are relaxed and fill with blood. Ventricles are also relaxed.
2. *Atrial systole* – Atria contract. Blood is pushed into the ventricles through the atrioventricular valves (bicuspid & tricuspid). Ventricles are relaxed.
3. *Ventricular systole* –Ventricles contract. Blood is pushed away from the heart through the pulmonary arteries and the aorta. Atria are relaxed.

1. The **a**_____ fill with blood.
LHS: o_____ blood from the pulmonary **v**_____.
RHS: d_____ blood from the **v**_____ **c**_____.

2. The wall of the atria **c**_____, this is known as atrial **s**_____. Blood is

forced by high pressure through the **atrioventricular valves** into the ventricles.

LHS = **b**_____ or mitral valve, RHS = **t**_____ valve.

3. The **v**_____ walls then contract: ventricular **s**_____.
The ventricular pressure increases and blood is forced through the **s**_____-**l**_____ valves.
LHS-**a**_____ **s**____ -**l**_____ **valve** opens to the **a**_____, **oxygenated** blood flows to the **body.**

RHS-**pulmonary s**_____-**l**_____ **valve** opens into the **p**_____ **a**_____, **deoxygenated** blood flows to the **lungs**.

The pressure in the ventricles decreases marking the **d**_____ **phase**. Atria begin to refill with blood.

Atrial pressure increases until the **a**_____ valves open and the cycle repeats.

Section 1: body systems

1a: The circulatory system

Learning outcomes:

* Describe the double circulatory system;
* Identify the main structures in the mammalian heart;
* Describe how the cardiac cycle is coordinated;
* **Explain the role of the SAN, AVN, Bundle of His & Purkinje fibres in the control of the cardiac cycle;**

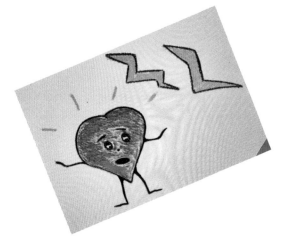

Match the parts of the heart to their function.

Purkinje fibres	The impulse passes down these nerve fibres where it reaches the ventricles.
Bundle of His	The signal passes here from across the atria where it is slowed down to allow the atria to contract together **(atrial systole).**
Sinoatrial node (SAN)	These nerve fibres spread the impulse across the ventricles causing them to contract **(ventricular systole).**
Atrioventricular node (AVN)	Initiates the electrical impulse that controls the heartbeat.

Across
2. Name of the artery leaving the left side of the heart.
5. The name of the valve separating the left atrium & left ventricle.
8. Type of blood vessel that has valves to prevent backflow of blood.
10. Name of the artery leaving the right side of the heart.
12. Name of the vein entering the right side of the heart.
14. Type of cells that line the lumen of each blood vessel.

Down
1. Name of the muscle tissue found in the heart.
3. Name of the bundle of nervous tissue that initiates the cardiac cycle.
4. Name of the nerve fibres that stimulate contraction of the ventricles.
6. Name of the vein entering the left side of the heart.
7. Valves that prevent backflow of blood into the ventricles.
9. Blood containing high levels of oxygen.
11. Type of circulatory system seen in birds & mammals.
13. Type of blood vessel that carries blood away from the heart.
15. The type of circulatory system commonly seen in invertebrates.

1b: The respiratory system

Learning outcomes:

* **Recall the names of the organs in the respiratory system;**
* Describe the function of the respiratory system;
* Describe how the process of gas exchange takes place;

Label the diagram below using the key words to help.

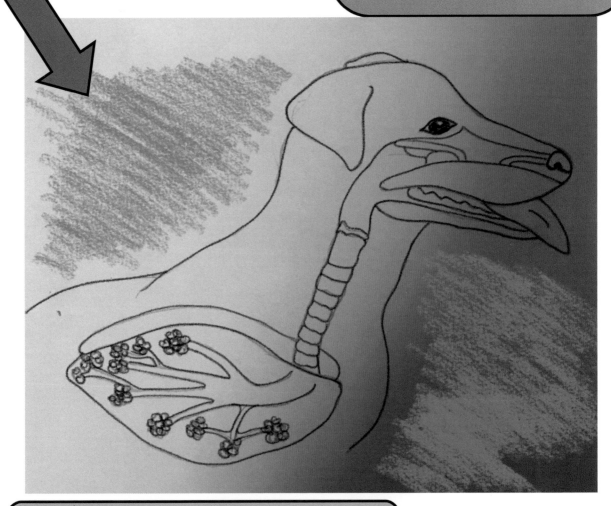

Key words:

Lung   Alveoli   Bronchi   Bronchioles   Trachea   Larynx
Pharynx   Nasal cavity   Turbinate bones

Section 1: body systems

1b: The respiratory system

Learning outcomes:

* Recall the names of the organs in the respiratory system;
* **Describe the function of the respiratory system;**
* Describe how the process of gas exchange takes place;

Copy the cards below to create a 'mix & match' card sort activity. Make sure you can match the function & structure to the correct parts of the respiratory system.

Part of respiratory system	Function	Structure
Nose & mouth	Allows air into the nasal cavity. Chemicals in the air bind to receptors in the olfactory epithelium, creating a sense of smell. Air passes on to the trachea.	Highly sensitive in many animal species the nasal cavity has a large surface area to increase the amount of air that can be breathed in & out.
Larynx	The 'voice box', allows animals to use sound to communicate. Connects the mouth & nose to the trachea allowing air to enter and leave.	A tube structure kept open by rings of cartilage.
Trachea	Connecting the larynx & pharynx to the lungs the trachea allows air to pass into and out of the lungs.	Kept open by rigid rings of cartilage. Lined with ciliated epithelial cells & goblet cells. Mucus is produced by the goblet cells which helps trap particles of dust & bacteria, preventing them from entering the lungs. Cilia then move the mucus out of the respiratory system.
Bronchi	Left & right bronchi allow air to pass into the left & right lungs.	Two tubes that branch off from the trachea. Similar in structure to the trachea they contain cartilage but also a small amount of smooth muscle.
Bronchioles	Creating a large surface area the bronchioles take air deeper into the lungs to the alveoli.	Smaller, branching tubes that go deep into the lungs. Containing no cartilage they are surrounded by smooth muscle which can contract & relax to control airflow.
Alveoli	Millions of alveoli in the lungs allow gas exchange to happen. Oxygen diffuses into the blood stream & carbon dioxide diffuses out.	Alveoli are only one cell thick. They are lined with squamous (squashed) epithelial cells. They have an excellent blood supply & a very large surface area to make gas exchange highly efficient.

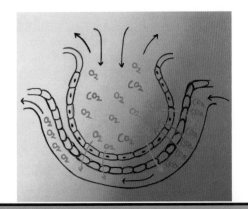

Learning outcomes:

* Recall the names of the organs in the respiratory system;
* Describe the function of the respiratory system;
* **Describe how the process of gas exchange takes place;**

Find the key words hidden in the word search below. Use these words to create a series of sentences describing the process of gas exchange.

A	S	A	T	H	X	C	O	P	C	E	G	A	I	R	S	A	C	S	D
W	L	S	B	N	F	I	O	J	A	K	G	H	L	D	F	B	I	O	T
S	D	V	T	A	B	V	N	M	R	K	R	E	Q	U	J	H	J	J	G
X	S	K	E	L	M	G	H	T	B	Y	P	O	F	R	S	G	R	H	T
Z	B	V	G	O	H	J	E	R	O	D	F	O	P	J	G	L	D	F	E
I	O	B	P	I	L	H	R	J	N	V	B	C	N	S	N	D	E	W	H
E	A	R	B	G	H	I	N	N	D	F	D	L	B	Y	U	D	F	O	L
P	E	O	Y	R	F	G	J	K	I	M	B	G	O	G	L	D	S	E	O
Q	A	N	S	Y	T	U	I	H	O	C	V	D	F	O	P	L	J	U	I
C	X	C	S	D	R	S	L	P	X	U	I	O	R	F	D	H	N	H	B
D	M	H	T	S	A	F	S	U	I	O	Z	D	J	P	D	F	H	K	J
N	K	I	R	A	C	R	H	S	D	P	X	G	K	L	G	I	L	L	S
T	L	O	F	T	H	E	R	D	E	L	V	Z	T	E	G	M	T	I	O
R	F	L	G	E	E	Q	F	R	M	D	I	D	Y	Q	I	L	Q	G	L
A	G	E	J	A	A	W	V	E	D	E	L	H	N	T	J	F	I	G	H
E	H	S	U	R	F	A	C	E	A	R	E	A	C	E	K	G	I	H	D
T	I	D	B	O	M	L	C	O	C	O	K	S	B	N	L	Y	P	F	F
R	O	I	N	P	N	O	J	P	F	N	E	G	Y	X	O	E	Y	S	A
H	D	O	F	L	U	Y	N	L	T	S	H	G	V	H	D	R	G	P	P
J	R	J	G	H	H	F	H	K	U	C	K	T	F	U	N	W	B	F	H

ALVEOLI	BRONCHI	AIR SACS	TRACHEA
LUNGS	BRONCHIOLES	GILLS	SURFACE AREA
BLOOD	CARBON DIOXIDE	OXYGEN	

1c: The reproductive system

Learning outcomes:

* **Identify the main organs in the male & female mammalian reproductive systems;**
* Describe the structure & function of the main organs in the mammalian reproductive systems;
* Describe the stages of the mammalian oestrus cycle;
* Recall the main hormones involved in the oestrus cycle & describe their function;

Label the organs of the female canine reproductive system.

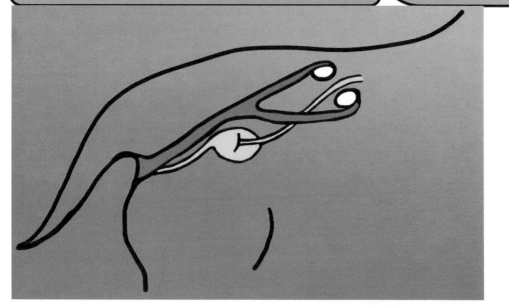

Label the organs of the male canine reproductive system.

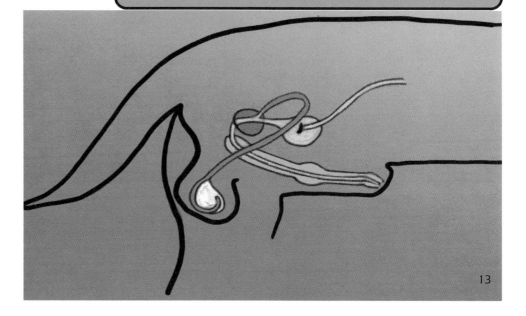

1c: The reproductive system

Learning outcomes:

* Identify the main organs in the male & female mammalian reproductive systems;
* **Describe the structure & function of the main organs in the mammalian reproductive systems;**
* Describe the stages of the mammalian oestrus cycle;
* Recall the main hormones involved in the oestrus cycle & describe their function;

Match the organs of the canine reproductive systems to their structure & function.

Ovaries	Narrow opening between the vagina and the uterus.	Place where sperm can enter the female during mating.
Uterus	External opening of the urogenital tract.	Produce eggs through the process of oogenesis. Oestrogen is also produced here.
Vagina	Females have two of these. Eggs grow within a follicle until mature. Small organs located on each side of the uterus in the pelvic cavity.	Enlarges when the female is in oestrus as a visual stimulant.
Cervix	Made up of the horns, body and cervix. Thick muscular walls called endometrium, helps support a fertilised egg.	Holds a fertilised egg in place during implantation and development through gestation.
Vulva	Tube creating an acidic environment to prevent infection.	Acts as a plug to prevent pathogens entering the uterus. Dilates during parturition to allow offspring to pass.
Scrotum	Small gland which produces semen.	Carries sperm out of the body. Also carries urine out of the body.
Penis	Covered in elastic skin called the prepuce or sheath.	Sperm are produced here through the process of spermatogenesis. This takes place within the seminiferous tubules via meiosis. Spermatogonium 'baby sperm' pass to the epididymis where they mature and become motile. Testosterone is also produced here.
Vas deferens	Located within the scrotum outside of the body to maintain optimum temperature.	Fluid which buffers the acidity of the vagina, acts as a medium to transport sperm and contains sugars as a source of energy for sperm.
Testes	Also known as the sperm duct. A narrow muscular tube.	Muscles help to raise and lower the testes to keep them at the optimum temperature.
Prostate gland	Thin tube-like structure.	Contains many blood vessels to become erect so it can enter the vagina.
Urethra	Contains the testes, large sac-like structure.	Sperm travel through from the testes to the urethra.

1c: The reproductive system

* Identify the main organs in the male & female mammalian reproductive systems;
* Describe the structure & function of the main organs in the mammalian reproductive systems;
* **Describe the stages of the mammalian oestrus cycle;**
* Recall the main hormones involved in the oestrus cycle & describe their function;

Put the stages of the canine oestrus cycle in the correct order.

Oestrus:
Lasts approx. 7 days
Will **accept** the male
Discharge decreases
LH levels peak stimulating ovulation.
Empty follicle dries up and becomes a **Corpus luteum.**
Progesterone levels increase.
Oestrogen levels decrease.

Metoestrus/dioestrus
Lasts approx. **55 days**
If fertilisation occurs lasts until pups are born.
Prolactin & oxytocin secreted towards the end of gestation.
Progesterone levels remain high. **LH & FSH** are inhibited.

Proestrus:
Lasts approx. 7 days
Growing follicle releases **oestrogen** from the ovary.
Female will attract a male but is **not yet receptive.**
Signs include **vulva swelling** & a **blood-tinged discharge.**

Anoestrus:
Lasts approx. **4 months**
Limited or **no hormonal** activity.

Late anoestrus:
GnRH released from the hypothalamus.
Stimulates **FSH & LH** production from the pituitary gland.
Stimulates an **oocyte (egg)** to **grow** inside the ovarian follicle.

1d: The urinary system

Learning outcomes:

* **Identify the main organs in the urinary system;**
* **Describe the structure & function of each organ;**
* Describe how the kidneys filter blood to produce urine;

Label the organs of the mammalian urinary system shown below.

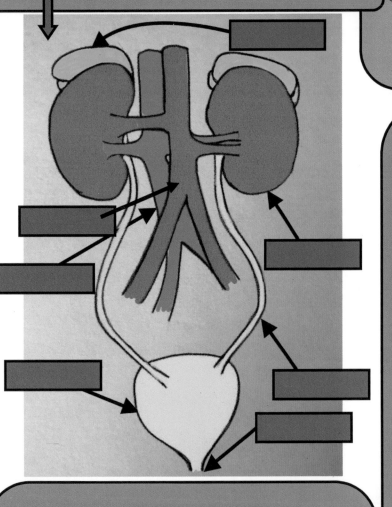

Write out descriptions of the structure & function of each part of the urinary system:

Organ	Structure	Function

Write definitions for the following key words:

Ultra-filtration:

Selective reabsorption:

Osmoregulation:

Homeostasis:

Kidney:

Urea:

Excretion:

Filtrate:

Osmosis:

Concentration gradient:

Counter-current multiplier:

Label the parts of the mammalian kidney shown below.

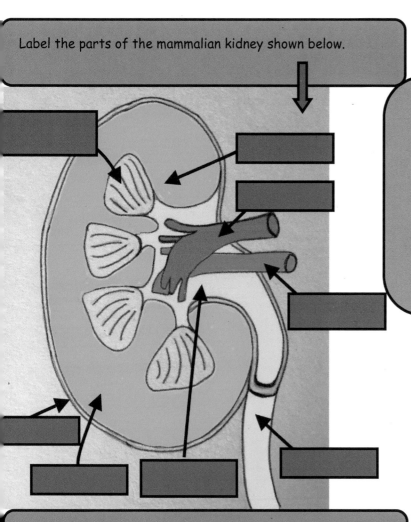

Label the parts of the nephron shown below. Use the key terms to describe how blood is filtered by the kidneys & urine is produced.

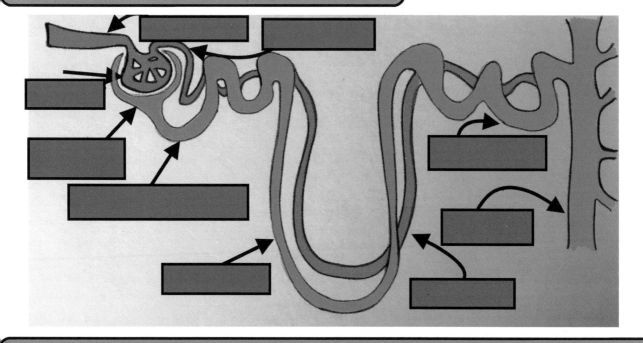

Key terms: Bowman's capsule, loop of Henle, proximal convoluted tubule, distal convoluted tubule, collecting duct, glomerulus.

1e: The musculoskeletal system

Learning outcomes:

* Recall the functions of the musculoskeletal system;
* Identify the main bones in a mammalian skeleton;
* Describe how the skeletons of different mammals are adapted for running, hopping, flying & swimming;

* Identify the bones shared between the different mammals.
* Make lists of how each animal is adapted for a specific type of movement: running, hopping, flying & swimming.

Dog

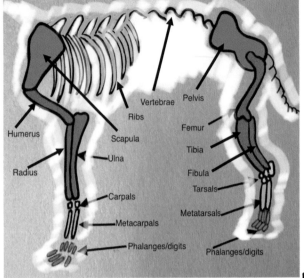

Vertebrae, Ribs, Scapula, Humerus, Radius, Ulna, Carpals, Metacarpals, Phalanges/digits, Pelvis, Femur, Tibia, Fibula, Tarsals, Metatarsals, Phalanges/digits

Bat

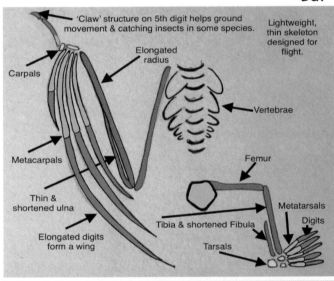

'Claw' structure on 5th digit helps ground movement & catching insects in some species.

Lightweight, thin skeleton designed for flight.

Elongated radius, Vertebrae, Carpals, Metacarpals, Thin & shortened ulna, Elongated digits form a wing, Femur, Tibia & shortened Fibula, Tarsals, Metatarsals, Digits

Rabbit

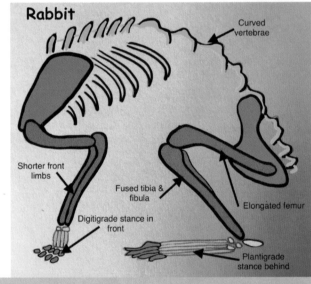

Curved vertebrae, Shorter front limbs, Fused tibia & fibula, Elongated femur, Digitigrade stance in front, Plantigrade stance behind

Whale

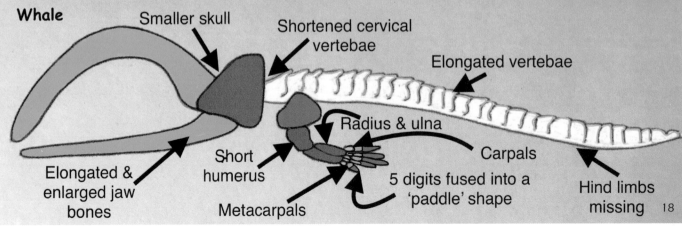

Smaller skull, Shortened cervical vertebae, Elongated vertebae, Radius & ulna, Carpals, Elongated & enlarged jaw bones, Short humerus, Metacarpals, 5 digits fused into a 'paddle' shape, Hind limbs missing

18

Similarities	Differences

Adaptations for movement:

Running

Swimming

Hopping

Flying

2a: Chemical control

Learning outcomes:

*   Define the term hormone;
*   Identify the main endocrine glands & state the hormones produced;
*   Describe how hormones control blood glucose levels;

A hormone is...

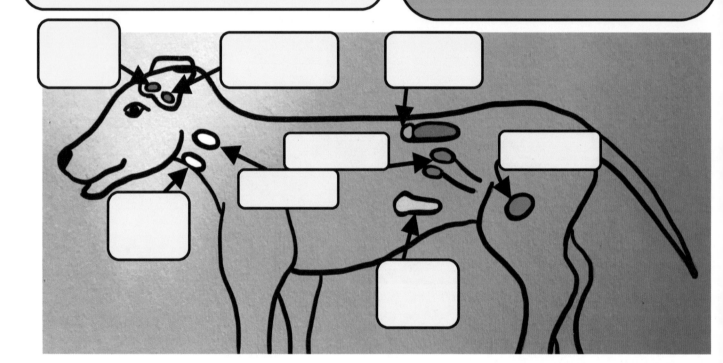

Name of endocrine gland	Hormone produced

2a: Chemical control

Learning outcomes:

* Define the term hormone;
* Identify the main endocrine glands & state the hormones produced;
* **Describe how hormones control blood glucose levels;**

Put the descriptions in the correct order to describe glucose control.

Glucose levels start to drop e.g. after a period of sleep/fasting.

Change is detected by receptor cells in the pancreas. Beta (β) cells of the islets of Langerhans release insulin into the blood.

Glucagon has several important effects on the body:
- Glycogen is converted to glucose & released from muscles & the liver.
- Fat can also be converted into glucose and released into the blood.
- Protein can be broken down and converted into glucose.

Change is detected by receptor cells in the pancreas. Alpha (α) cells of the islets of Langerhans release glucagon into the blood.

Blood glucose levels rise e.g. after eating.

Insulin has several important effects on the body:
- Glucose is converted to glycogen and stored in the liver & muscles.
- Glucose can be converted into fat & stored.
- Cells absorb more glucose for respiration.

Glucose returns to a safe level.

2b: Temperature control

Learning outcomes:

Define the terms endothermic & ectothermic;
Describe how endothermic animals regulate their body temperature;
Describe how ectothermic animals regulate their body temperature;

Fill in the missing information below. Use this information to describe how endotherms regulate their body temperature.

Endothermic:

Ectothermic:

Falling blood temperature

Blood temperature falls

Blood temperature rises

Negative feedback loop

Rising blood temperature

Blood temperature rises

Blood temperature falls

Negative feedback loop

Temperature control in ectotherms

B_____ in the sun

Increased b_____, increasing heat loss via e_____

Finding s_____

C_____: gaining heat via warm objects (sitting on a warm rock)

Cooling in w_____

22

2c: Neural control

Learning outcomes:

Identify the main areas of the mammalian brain;
Describe some of the main functions of each area of the brain;
Identify the components of the somatic & autonomic nervous system;
Describe the effects of the sympathetic & parasympathetic nervous system;

Label the diagram below to identify the main areas of the mammalian brain.

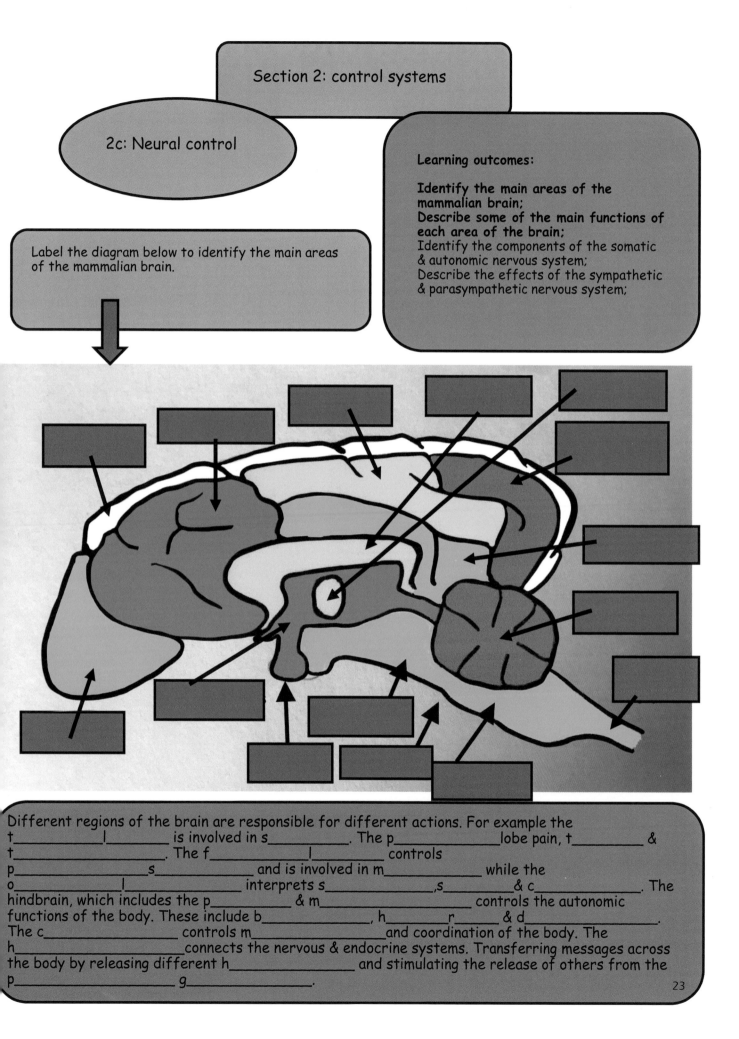

Different regions of the brain are responsible for different actions. For example the
t_____l_____ is involved in s_____. The p_____lobe pain, t_____ &
t_____. The f_____l_____ controls
p_____s_____ and is involved in m_____ while the
o_____l_____ interprets s_____,s_____ & c_____. The
hindbrain, which includes the p_____ & m_____ controls the autonomic
functions of the body. These include b_____, h_____r_____ & d_____.
The c_____ controls m_____and coordination of the body. The
h_____connects the nervous & endocrine systems. Transferring messages across
the body by releasing different h_____ and stimulating the release of others from the
p_____ g_____.

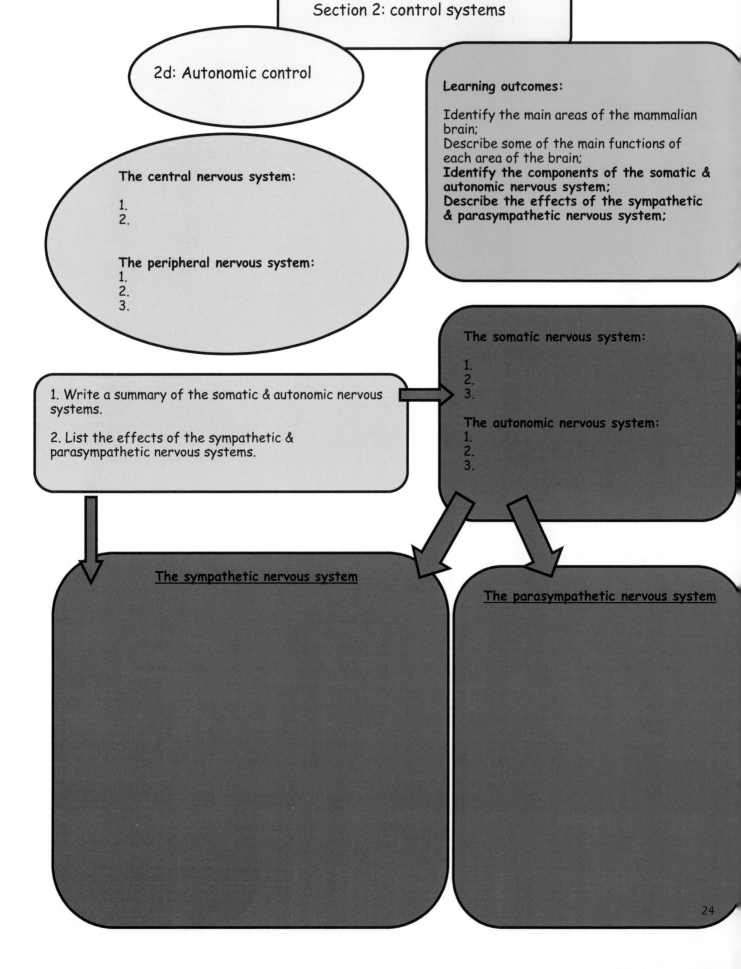

Section 2: control systems

2d: Autonomic control

Learning outcomes:

Identify the main areas of the mammalian brain;
Describe some of the main functions of each area of the brain;
Identify the components of the somatic & autonomic nervous system;
Describe the effects of the sympathetic & parasympathetic nervous system;

The central nervous system:

1.
2.

The peripheral nervous system:
1.
2.
3.

The somatic nervous system:

1.
2.
3.

The autonomic nervous system:
1.
2.
3.

1. Write a summary of the somatic & autonomic nervous systems.

2. List the effects of the sympathetic & parasympathetic nervous systems.

<u>The sympathetic nervous system</u>

<u>The parasympathetic nervous system</u>

3a: The eye

Learning outcomes:

Identify the main components of the mammalian eye;
Describe the structure & function of each component;
Describe some of the extra sensory adaptations seen in animals;

1. Identify & label each component of the eye.

2. Write a brief description of the structure & function of each component.

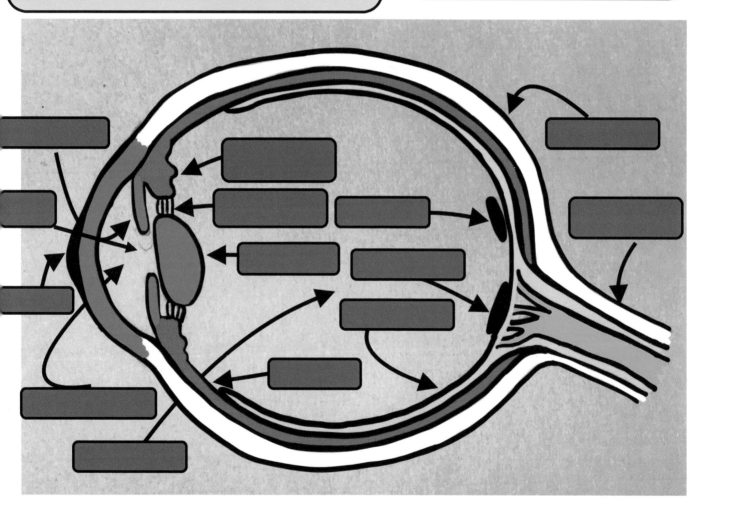

Write a summary of each component here.

3b: The ear

Learning outcomes:

Identify the main components of the mammalian ear;
Describe the structure & function of each component;
Describe some of the extra sensory adaptations seen in animals;

1. Identify & label each component of the ear

2. Write a brief description of the structure & function of each component.

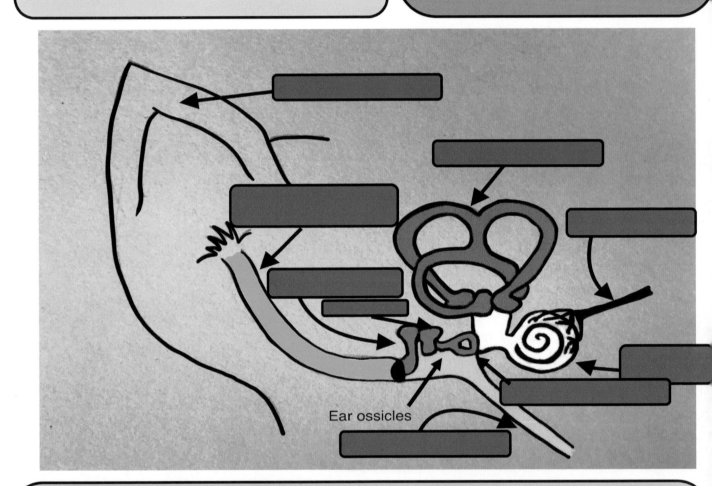

Ear ossicles

Write a summary of each component here.

3c: The olfactory system

Learning outcomes:

Identify the main components of the mammalian nose;
Describe the structure & function of each component;
Describe some of the extra sensory adaptations seen in animals;

1. Identify & label each component of the olfactory system.

2. Write a brief description of the structure & function of each component.

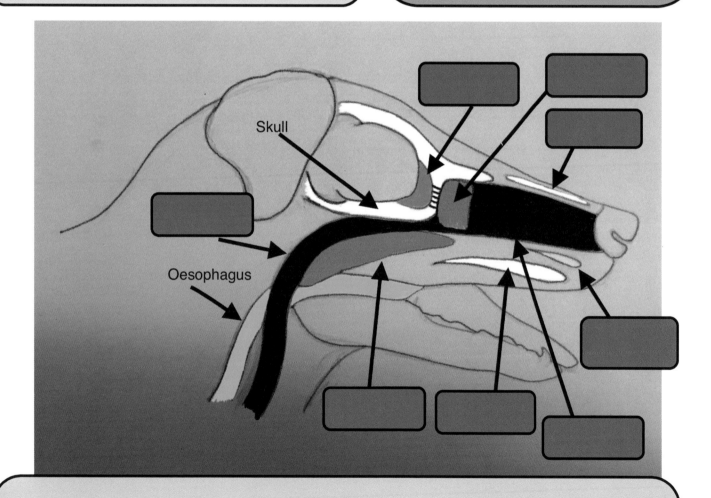

Skull

Oesophagus

Write a summary of each component here.

3d: The mouth

Learning outcomes:

Identify the main components of the mammalian taste bud ;
Describe the structure & function of each component;
Describe some of the extra sensory adaptations seen in animals;

1. Identify & label each component of the taste bud.

2. Write a brief description of the structure & function of each component.

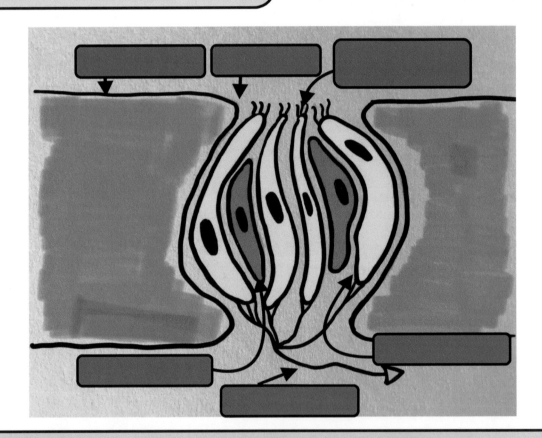

Write a summary of each component here.

3e: The skin

Learning outcomes:

Identify the main components of the mammalian skin;
Describe the structure & function of each component;
Describe some of the extra sensory adaptations seen in animals;

1. Identify & label each component of the skin.

2. Write a brief description of the structure & function of each component.

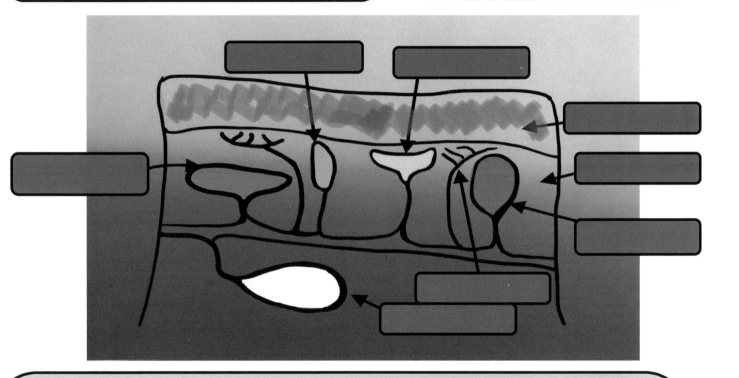

Write a summary of each component here.

4a: Special adaptations

Learning outcomes:

Describe some of the extra sensory adaptations seen in animals;

Match the sensory adaptations to their correct description & examples of animals.

Name of adaptation	Description	Example of animals
Tapetum lucidum	Only works in animals that live in/near water. Specially adapted receptors known as Ampullae of Lorenzini, located around the nose & mouth can detect very weak electromagnetic fields that are produced by living organisms. This allows the animal to effectively find prey.	Horses, snakes, dogs, cats
Jacobson's organ	High frequency sound waves are emitted. The animal uses the echoes of the sound waves reflected off of nearby objects to determine direction, distance & speed in order to find prey, navigate & orientate themselves.	Dogs, cats, horses, deer
Electroreception	A specialised chemoreceptor found in many mammal species. Used to detect chemicals in the environment such as pheromones. Used by animals to communicate, often associated with readiness for reproduction. May also be used in determining aggressive tendencies & territorial disputes. Can also be used to detect prey.	Bats, toothed whales, dolphins
Echolocation	An extra layer at the back of the eye that sits behind the retina. It reflects additional light onto the retina which helps to improve vision, particularly at night. Seen in both predator & prey species, often either nocturnal or crepuscular animals.	Sharks & platypus

Section 4: sensory adaptations

4b: Predator/prey adaptations

Learning outcomes:

Compare the sensory adaptations of predators and prey;

Use this table to compare the sensory organs of predators & prey.

Predators	Prey

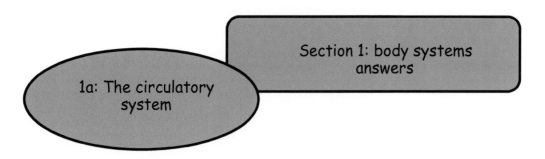

The double circulatory system

The **MAMMALIAN** heart is described as a **DOUBLE** circulatory system because the heart has two separated halves. The left side pumps **OXYGENATED** blood and the right side **DEOXYGENATED** blood.

The left side of the heart pumps blood from the heart to various **TISSUES** and **ORGANS** in the body (**systemic** circulation) and the smaller, right hand side of the heart pumps blood to the **LUNGS** (**pulmonary** circulation).

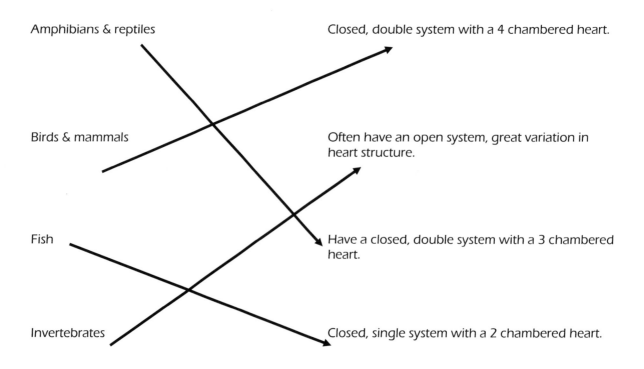

The circulatory systems consists of the **HEART** veins, arteries & capillaries.

Animals such as **CATS** and **DOGS** have a **DOUBLE CIRCULATORY** system.

This means blood travels more efficiently round the body, transporting more O_2 & **GLUCOSE** to the body cells.

The mammalian **HEART** consists of **FOUR** chambers.

Some animals like **FISH** have a **SINGLE CIRCULATORY** system with only 2 chambers.

Draw 2 simple diagrams to show how a single & double circulatory system works.

Single

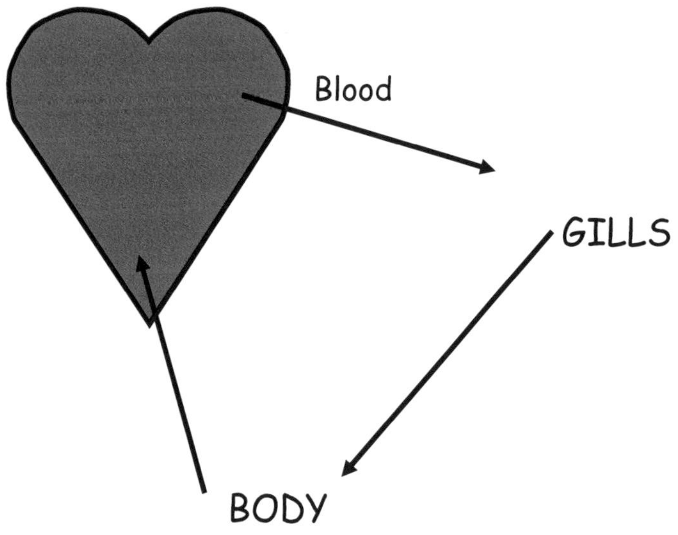

Double

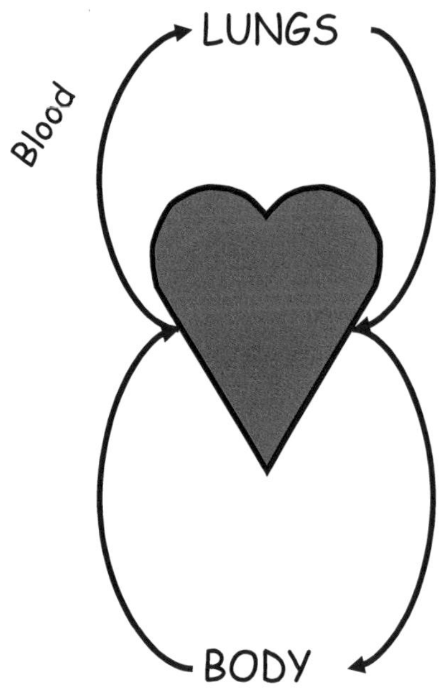

1. The **ATRIA** fill with blood.

LHS: **OXYGENATED** blood from the pulmonary **VEIN**.

RHS: **DEOXYGENATED** blood from the **VENA CAVA.**

2. The wall of the atria **CONTRACT**, this is known as atrial **SYSTOLE**. Blood is forced by high pressure through the **atrioventricular valves** into the ventricles.

LHS = **BICUSPID** or mitral valve, RHS = **TRICUSPID** valve.

3. The **VENTRICLE** walls then contract; ventricular **SYSTOLE.**

The ventricular pressure increases and blood is forced through the **SEMI-LUNAR** valves.

LHS- **AORTIC SEMI-LUNAR** valve opens to the **AORTA, oxygenated** blood flows to the **body.**

RHS-**pulmonary SEMI-LUNAR** valve opens into the **PULMONARY ARTERY, deoxygenated** blood flows to **lungs.**

The pressure in the ventricles decreases marking the **DIASTOLE** phase. Atria begin to refill with blood.

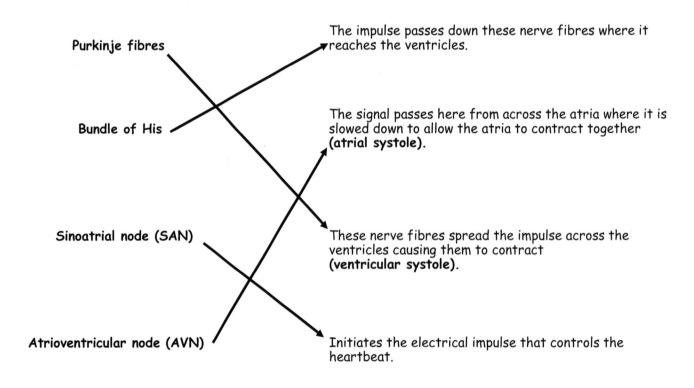

Purkinje fibres

Bundle of His

Sinoatrial node (SAN)

Atrioventricular node (AVN)

The impulse passes down these nerve fibres where it reaches the ventricles.

The signal passes here from across the atria where it is slowed down to allow the atria to contract together (atrial systole).

These nerve fibres spread the impulse across the ventricles causing them to contract (ventricular systole).

Initiates the electrical impulse that controls the heartbeat.

Across

2. Name of the artery leaving the left side of the heart.
5. The name of the valve separating the left atrium & left ventricle.
8. Type of blood vessel that has valves to prevent backflow of blood.
10. Name of the artery leaving the right side of the heart.
12. Name of the vein entering the right side of the heart.
14. Type of cells that line the lumen of each blood vessel.

Down

1. Name of the muscle tissue found in the heart.
3. Name of the bundle of nervous tissue that initiates the cardiac cycle.
4. Name of the nerve fibres that stimulate contraction of the ventricles.
6. Name of the vein entering the left side of the heart.
7. Valves that prevent backflow of blood into the ventricles.
9. Blood containing high levels of oxygen.
11. Type of circulatory system seen in birds & mammals.
13. Type of blood vessel that carries blood away from the heart.
15. The type of circulatory system commonly seen in invertebrates.

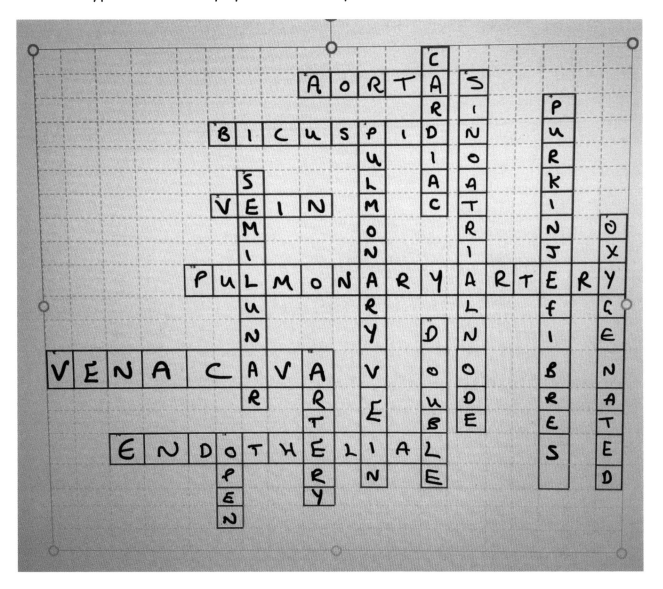

1b: The respiratory
system

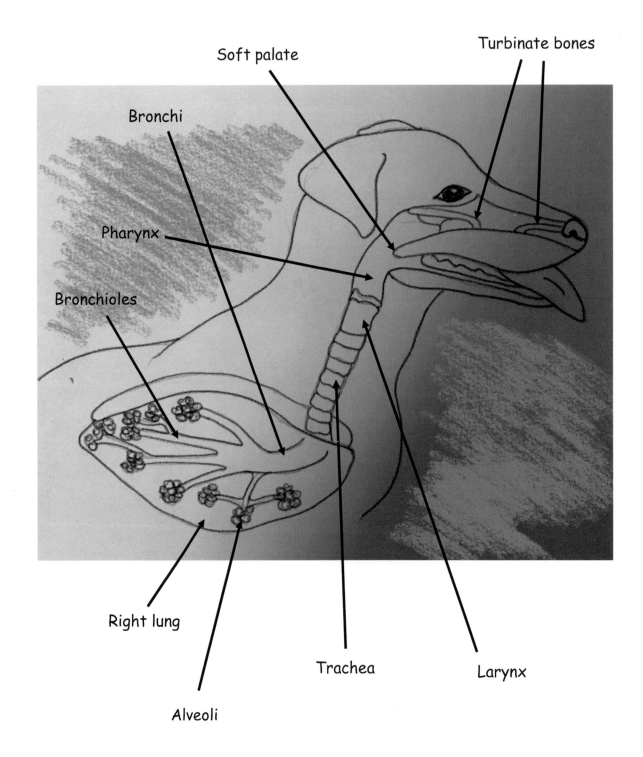

Soft palate

Turbinate bones

Bronchi

Pharynx

Bronchioles

Right lung

Trachea

Larynx

Alveoli

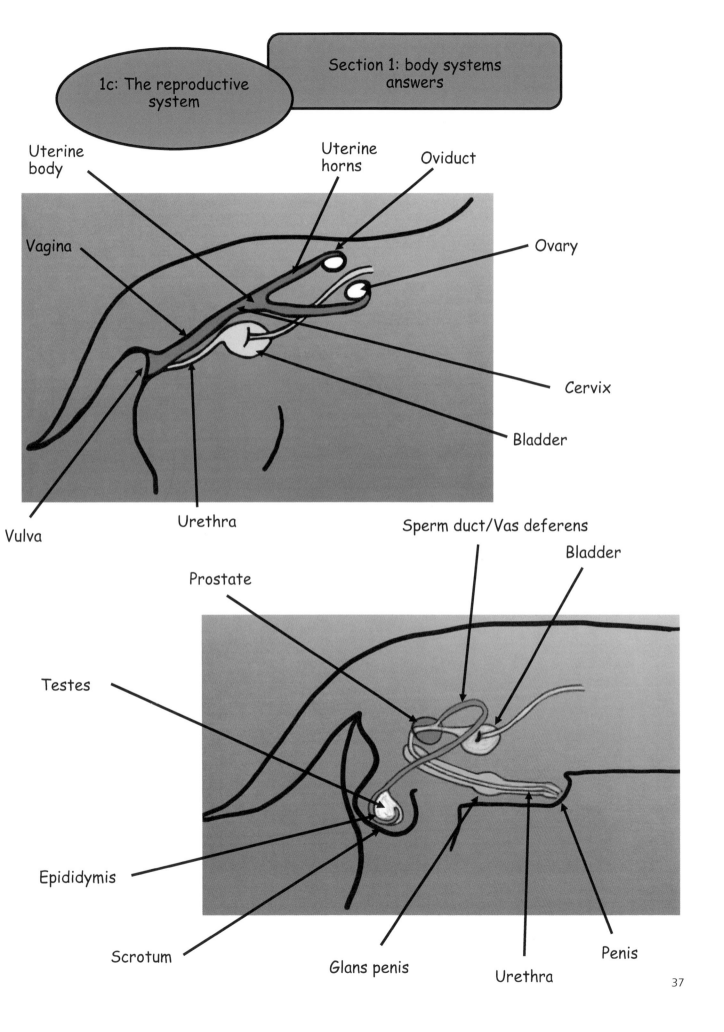

Uterine body

Uterine horns

Oviduct

Ovary

Vagina

Cervix

Bladder

Vulva

Urethra

Sperm duct/Vas deferens

Bladder

Prostate

Testes

Epididymis

Scrotum

Glans penis

Urethra

Penis

Organ	Structure	Function
Ovaries	Females have two of these. Eggs grow within a follicle until mature. Small organs located on each side of the uterus in the pelvic cavity.	Produce eggs through the process of oogenesis. Oestrogen is also produced here.
Uterus	Made up of the horns, body and cervix. Thick muscular walls called endometrium, helps support a fertilised egg.	Holds a fertilised egg in place during implantation and development through gestation.
Vagina	Tube creating an acidic environment to prevent infection.	Place where sperm can enter the female during mating.
Cervix	Narrow opening between the vagina and the uterus.	Acts as a plug to prevent pathogens entering the uterus. Dilates during parturition to allow offspring to pass.
Vulva	External opening of the urogenital tract.	Enlarges when female is in oestrus as visual stimulant.

Organ	Structure	Function
Scrotum	Contains the testes, large sac-like structure.	Muscles help to raise and lower the testes to keep them at the optimum temperature.
Penis	Covered in elastic skin called the prepuce or sheath.	Contains many blood vessels to become erect so it can enter the vagina.
Vas deferens	Also known as the sperm duct. A narrow muscular tube.	Sperm travel through from the testes to the urethra.
Testes	Located within the scrotum outside of the body to maintain optimum temperature.	Sperm are produced here through the process of spermatogenesis. This takes place within the seminiferous tubules via meiosis. Spermatogonium 'baby sperm' pass to the epididymis where they mature and become motile. Testosterone is also produced here.
Prostate gland	Small gland which produces semen.	Fluid which buffers the acidity of the vagina, acts as a medium to transport sperm and contains sugars as a source of energy for sperm.
Urethra	Thin tube-like structure.	Carries sperm out of the body. Also carries urine out of the body.

Put the stages of the canine oestrus cycle in the correct order.

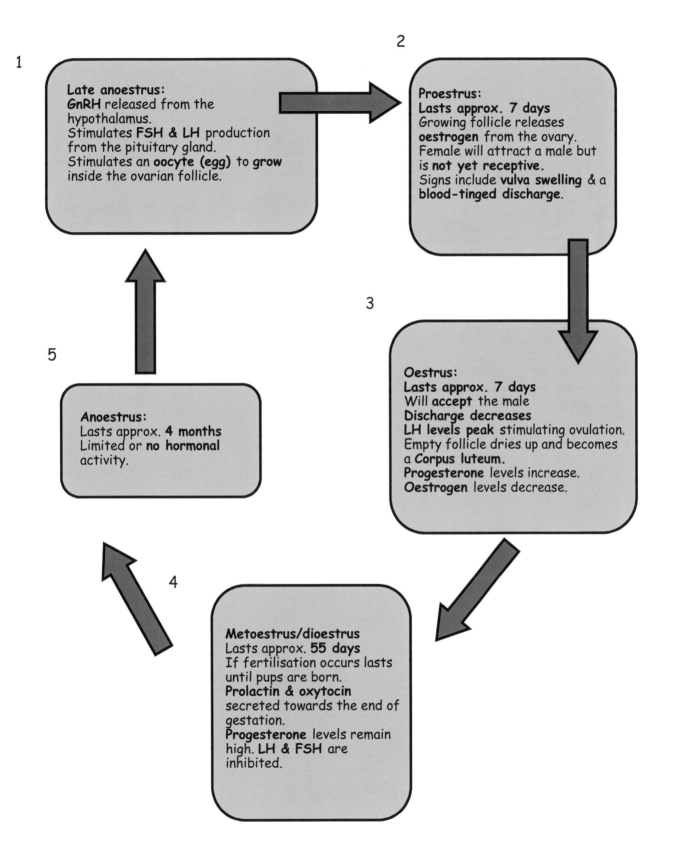

1

Late anoestrus:
GnRH released from the hypothalamus.
Stimulates FSH & LH production from the pituitary gland.
Stimulates an oocyte (egg) to grow inside the ovarian follicle.

2

Proestrus:
Lasts approx. 7 days
Growing follicle releases oestrogen from the ovary.
Female will attract a male but is not yet receptive.
Signs include vulva swelling & a blood-tinged discharge.

3

Oestrus:
Lasts approx. 7 days
Will accept the male
Discharge decreases
LH levels peak stimulating ovulation.
Empty follicle dries up and becomes a Corpus luteum.
Progesterone levels increase.
Oestrogen levels decrease.

4

Metoestrus/dioestrus
Lasts approx. 55 days
If fertilisation occurs lasts until pups are born.
Prolactin & oxytocin secreted towards the end of gestation.
Progesterone levels remain high. LH & FSH are inhibited.

5

Anoestrus:
Lasts approx. 4 months
Limited or no hormonal activity.

1d: The urinary system

Structure & function.

Label the organs of the mammalian urinary system shown below.

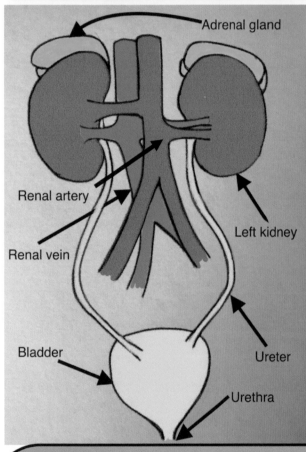

Adrenal gland

Renal artery

Renal vein

Left kidney

Bladder

Ureter

Urethra

Renal artery: Brings oxygenated blood into the kidney.
Renal vein: Removes deoxygenated blood from the kidney.
Ureter: Thin tubes that funnel urine from the kidneys into the bladder.
Bladder: Elastic organ that holds urine before it is removed from the body via the urethra.
Urethra: Thin tube that carries urine out of the body. Also carries semen out of the body in male mammals.
Kidneys: Organs located on either side of the spine in the abdomen. They filter blood to excrete excess water, salts & urea. Responsible for maintaining blood pressure as well as the correct balance of water & salts in the body.
Adrenal glands: Part of the endocrine system they produce hormones such as adrenaline & noradrenaline in response to signals from the nervous system.

Key word definitions:

Ultra-filtration: The process of all small molecules being removed from the blood stream. This process happens under high pressure in the glomerulus of the nephron.
Selective reabsorption: Selected molecules that are filtered out of the blood are then reabsorbed as they pass through the nephron. Molecules include glucose, water, salt ions and hormones.
Osmoregulation: The regulation of water & salt content in the blood.
Homeostasis: Regulation of internal body conditions such as temperature, blood pressure and pH.
Kidney: Bean-shaped organs that filter blood to remove excess water & salts. Also responsible for regulating blood pressure.
Urea: A waste product produced in the liver as a result of protein breakdown. Removed by the kidneys and excreted along with water as urine.
Excretion: The process of removing waste products from the body.
Filtrate: The solution formed in the nephron as a result of ultra-filtration.
Osmosis: The movement of water molecules down a concentration gradient through a partially permeable membrane.
Concentration gradient: The difference in the concentration of a solute between two regions of the body.
Counter-current multiplier: A mechanism within the kidney that produces a high concentration gradient in order to maximise reabsorption of water.

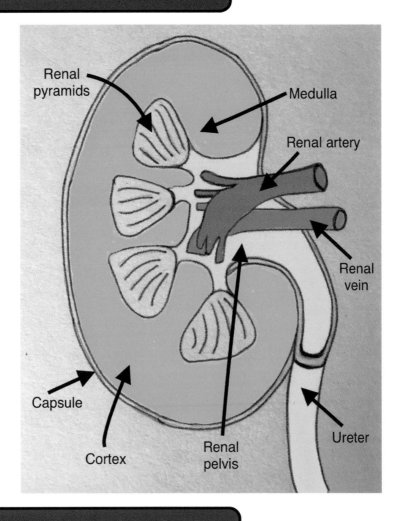

Renal pyramids

Medulla

Renal artery

Renal vein

Capsule

Cortex

Renal pelvis

Ureter

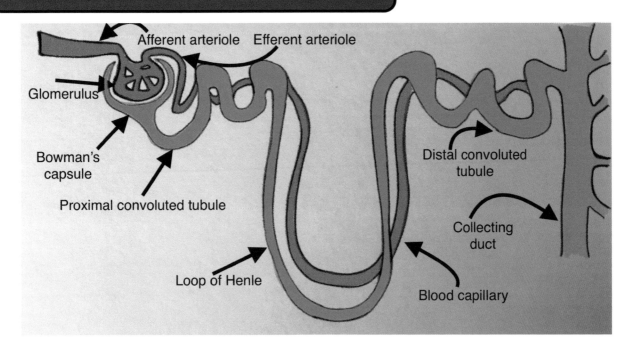

Afferent arteriole   Efferent arteriole

Glomerulus

Bowman's capsule

Proximal convoluted tubule

Distal convoluted tubule

Collecting duct

Loop of Henle

Blood capillary

Use key terms to describe how the kidneys filter blood and produce urine.

1. Blood enters the nephron through a **wide, afferent** arteriole. It then passes through the **glomerulus** (network of blood capillaries) at **high pressure**.
2. All small molecules are filtered out of the blood and pass into the **Bowman's capsule**. This **includes** water, urea, glucose, amino acids & hormones. It does **not include** larger molecules such as plasma proteins, red & white blood cells & platelets. Blood then flows out via the **smaller, efferent** arteriole.
3. Liquid in the Bowman's capsule is now called **glomerular filtrate**. This filtrate now passes to the **proximal convoluted tubule (PCT)**. Important solutes such as glucose are now **actively** transported back into the blood along with some water and other small molecules. This is known as **selective reabsorption**.
4. Filtrate then passes into the **loop of Henle**. As it moves down the **descending** loop **water** is reabsorbed into the blood via **osmosis**. Salts remain in the filtrate as the membrane of the descending loop is mostly **impermeable** to salt ions.
5. The remaining filtrate passes into the **ascending loop**. Here the membrane is impermeable to water. **Salt ions** are **actively** pumped out of the filtrate. These ions then diffuse across to the descending loop creating a **concentration gradient** between the filtrate & surrounding tissue fluid. This causes more water to be reabsorbed via osmosis. This process is called the **counter-current multiplier**.
6. Remaining filtrate passes to the **distal convoluted tubule (DCT)** and the **collecting duct**. Here further water can be reabsorbed into the blood, this is controlled by the action of a hormone known as **anti-diuretic hormone (ADH)**.
7. Excess water & urea pass down the collecting duct where it will drain into the **renal pelvis** and on to the **bladder** via the ureters where is it **excreted as urine** through the urethra.

1e: The musculoskeletal system

Similarities	Differences

Similarities

- All have several digits
- Same bones seen in the arms; radius, ulna, humerus.
- Same bones seen in the legs; tibia, fibula, femur.
- All have a tail (coccygeal vertebrae)
- All have the same sections of vertebrae: cervical, thoracic, lumbar, sacral & coccygeal.

Differences

- Horse has fused digits to form a single 'toe'
- Whale has digits fused into a 'paddle' shaped fin.
- Rabbit has curved vertebrae
- Rabbit has bent & elongated hind legs
- Whale has lost the hind limbs
- Whale lacks cervical vertebrae
- Whale has a small skull & enlarged jaw bones (baleen whales)
- Bat has elongated digits that form a wing
- Bat has legs turned out
- Horse/dog has long legs & large ribcage
- Several different walking styles: plantigrade (humans, rabbit hindlegs, kangaroo), digitigrade (dogs, cats, rabbit front legs) & unguligrade (horses, deer).

Adaptations for movement:

Running

Long legs, larger stride
Large ribcage, large lungs & heart
Front limbs are not attached directly to the skeleton, longer stride, faster running
Large nasal cavity, more oxygen, faster running
Horse—unguligrade/dog digitigrade, for greater stride length.

Swimming

Digits fused to form a fin, aids movement through the water
Hindlimbs lost, body more streamlined, faster swimming
Large jaws, large intake of food
Lack of cervical vertebrae, more streamlined shape
Shortened humerus, powerful movement of the fins.

Hopping

Hindlimbs bent, powerful push
Vertebrae curved, more force to hindlimbs
Back feet are 'plantigrade' larger surface area to give more push
Lightweight skeleton, faster movement
Hindlegs are longer than the front legs for more 'push' off the ground

Flying

Digits elongated to form a wing
Lightweight skeleton to aid flight
Hindlimbs turn out, can be tucked under to aid flight
5th digit 'claw' shape to allow hanging upside down. & capture of insects (in some species).

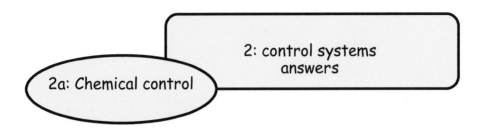
A hormone is... a chemical messenger that is carried in the bloodstream. They control the activity of specific cells or organs in the body. Secreted by endocrine glands.

Endocrine glands

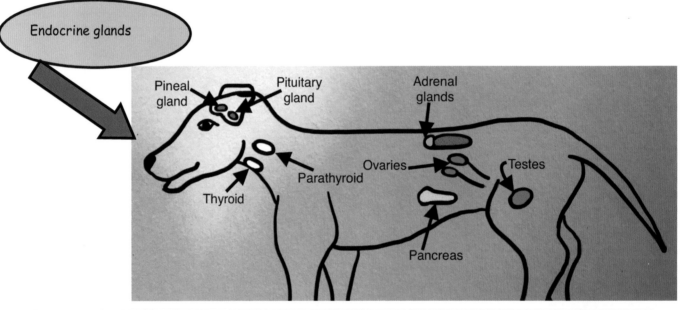

Endocrine gland	Hormone	Action
Pineal	melatonin	Regulates sleep
Pituitary or 'master gland'	ADH – Anti-diuretic hormone ACTH – adrenocorticotrophic hormone Oxytocin FSH – follicle stimulating hormone LH – luteinising hormone	Controls reabsorption of water Stimulates release of hormones from the adrenal glands. Contraction of smooth muscle in uterus, secretion of milk. Controls development of follicles in ovaries Stimulates ovulation& formation of corpus luteum.
Parathyroid	Parathyroid hormone	Control levels of calcium in blood
Thyroid	Thyroxine & triiodothyronine	Control metabolic rate & growth
Adrenal	Cortisol (cortex) Adrenaline/epinephrine (medulla) Noradrenaline/norepinephrine (medulla)	Raise blood glucose in response to stress. Prepares body for increased activity. Stimulates the Autonomic nervous system (sympathetic system). As for adrenaline.
Ovaries	Oestrogen Progesterone	Promotes female sex characteristics. Maintains pregnancy, inhibits FSH & LH.
Testes	Testosterone	Promotes male sex characteristics Supports sperm production
Pancreas	Insulin & glucagon	Controls blood glucose levels.

2: control systems answers

2a: Chemical control

Put the descriptions in the correct order to describe glucose control.

Blood glucose levels rise e.g. after eating.

Change is detected by receptor cells in the pancreas. Beta (β) cells of the islets of Langerhans release insulin into the blood.

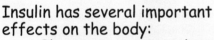

Insulin has several important effects on the body:
- Glucose is converted to glycogen and stored in the liver & muscles.
- Glucose can be converted into fat & stored.
- Cells absorb more glucose for respiration.

Glucose returns to a safe level.

Glucose levels start to drop e.g. after a period of sleep/fasting.

Change is detected by receptor cells in the pancreas. Alpha (α) cells of the islets of Langerhans release glucagon into the blood.

Glucagon has several important effects on the body:
- Glycogen is converted to glucose & released from muscles & the liver.
- Fat can also be converted into glucose and released into the blood.
- Protein can be broken down and converted into glucose.

Glucose returns to a safe level.

2b: Temperature control

Falling blood temperature

Detector cells in the hypothalamus

Blood temperature falls

Blood temperature rises

Negative feedback loop

Effectors
Decreased heat loss:
Skin arterioles – vasoconstriction.
Behavioural mechanisms
Hair erector muscles contract
Increased heat production:
Shivering
Respiration in brown fat (infants only)

Rising blood temperature

Detector cells in the hypothalamus

Blood temperature rises

Blood temperature falls

Negative feedback loop

Effectors
Increased heat loss:
Skin arterioles – vasodilation
Behavioural mechanisms
Sweating
Hair erector muscles relax
Decreased heat production:
Less respiration in brown fat

Temperature control in ectotherms

Cooling

Warming

Basking in the sun.

Increased **breathing,**
increasing heat loss via **evaporation.**

Finding **shade.**

Conduction: gaining heat via
warm objects (sitting on a warm rock).

Cooling in **water.**

2c: Neural control

Label the diagram below to identify the main areas of the mammalian brain.

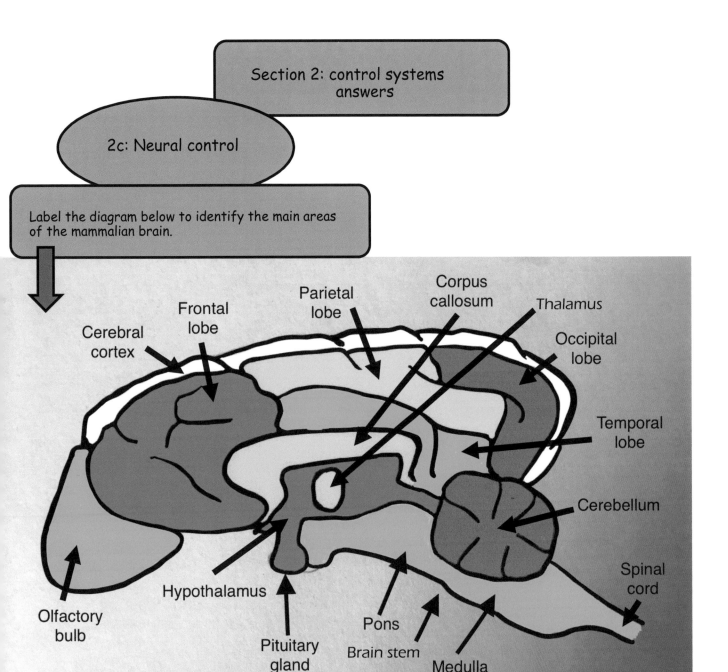

Frontal lobe

Parietal lobe

Corpus callosum

Thalamus

Cerebral cortex

Occipital lobe

Temporal lobe

Cerebellum

Spinal cord

Olfactory bulb

Hypothalamus

Pituitary gland

Pons

Brain stem

Medulla

Different regions of the brain are responsible for different actions. For example the **TEMPORAL LOBE** is involved in **SPEECH.** The **PARIETAL** lobe pain, **TOUCH & TEMPERATURE.** The **FRONTAL LOBE** controls **PROBLEM SOLVING** and is involved in **MEMORY** while the **OCCIPITAL LOBE** interprets **SIGHT, SHAPE & COLOUR**. The hindbrain, which includes the **PONS & MEDULLA** controls the autonomic functions of the body. These include **BREATHING, HEART RATE & DIGESTION.** The **CEREBELLUM** controls **MOVEMENT** and coordination of the body. The **HYPOTHALAMUS** connects the nervous & endocrine systems. Transferring messages across the body by releasing different **HORMONES** and stimulating the release of others from the **PITUITARY GLAND.**

2d: Autonomic control

The central nervous system:

1. Brain
2. Spinal cord

The peripheral nervous system:
1. Sensory (afferent) neurones
2. Motor (efferent) neurones
3. Ganglionic neurones

The somatic nervous system:

1. Under conscious control
2. Uses sensory (afferent) neurones to send impulses to the CNS.
3. Motor (efferent) neurones connect to skeletal muscle, sensory organs & skin.

The autonomic nervous system:
1. Not under conscious control.
2. Uses pre & postganglionic neurones which connect to areas of smooth muscle & glands.
3. Made up of two pathways:
A)   Sympathetic—fight or flight
B)   Parasympathetic—rest & digest

1. Write a summary of the somatic & autonomic nervous systems.

2. List the effects of the sympathetic & parasympathetic nervous systems.

Effects of the parasympathetic & sympathetic nervous systems

Sympathetic:
Causes adrenaline & noradrenaline to be released from the adrenal glands
Increases heart rate
Dilates pupils
Inhibits digestion
Relaxes airways
Stimulates production of & release of glucose.

Parasympathetic:
Inhibits release of adrenaline & noradrenaline
Reduces heart rate
Constricts pupils
Stimulates digestion & production of enzymes
Constricts airways
Stimulates release of insulin to return glucose level to normal range.

3a: The eye

1. Identify & label each component of the eye.

2. Write a brief description of the structure & function of each component.

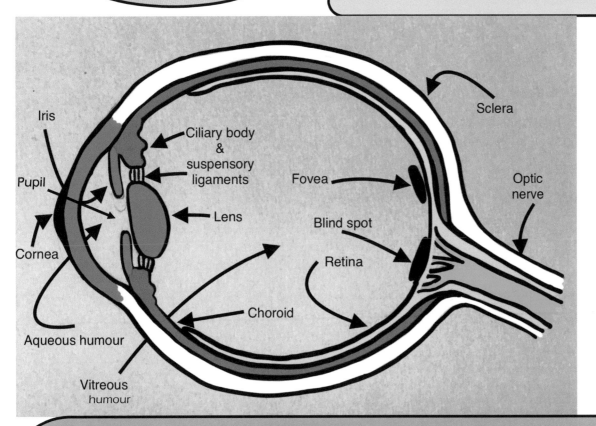

Iris

Ciliary body
&
suspensory
ligaments

Sclera

Pupil

Fovea

Optic
nerve

Lens

Blind spot

Cornea

Retina

Aqueous humour

Choroid

Vitreous
humour

Parts	Function
Cornea	Curves, protects the eye & helps to bend (refract) light as it enters the eye.
Pupil	Lets light enter the eye
Iris	Coloured smooth muscle, controls the size of the pupil.
Aqueous humour	Delivery of nutrients, expands cornea, refracts light
Ciliary muscle & suspensory ligaments	Work together to alter the shape of the lens to focus light on the retina.
Lens	Changes shape to refract light onto the retina
Vitreous humour	Keeps the shape of the eye. Delivery of nutrients
Retina	Contains rod & cone cells to detect light
Fovea	Concentrated area of cone cells
Rod & cone cells	Photoreceptors found on the retina. Stimulated by light & generate an electrical impulse. Rods are stimulated in low light levels, cone cells detect colour.
Choroid	Delivers oxygen & nutrients to the retina.
Sclera	White outer layer, tough for protection
Optic nerve	Connects neurones from receptors. Sends impulses to the brain.

3b: The ear

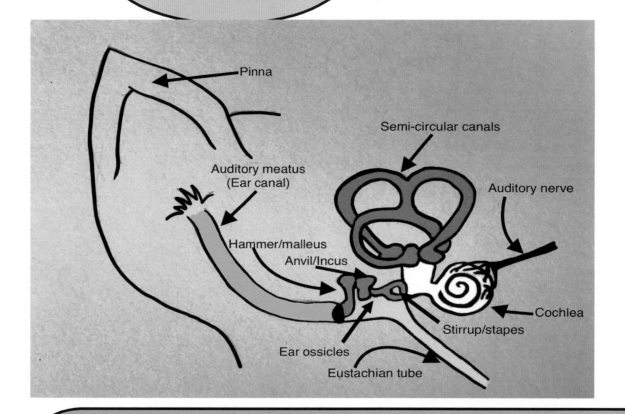

Part	Function
Pinna	External part of the ear, funnel sound waves into the ear.
Ear canal	Sound waves travel down here to the ear drum.
Ear drum/Tympanic membrane	Thin membrane that vibrates transferring sound waves to middle ear.
Ear ossicles (malleus, incus, stapes)	Vibrate, passing sound waves to inner ear.
Oval window	Separates middle & inner ear. Stapes passes vibrations to the oval window which, with the round window passes vibrations to the cochlea.
Cochlea	Vibrations pass to the cochlea: the organ of Corti within the cochlea transfers vibrations into an electrical impulse.
Semi-circular canals/vestibular organ	Respond to motion of the head & body. Responsible for balance. Sends impulses to the brain via the vestibular nerve.
Auditory nerve	Carries impulses to the brain from the cochlea.
Eustachian tube	Can open & close to control air pressure within the ear.

3c: The olfactory system

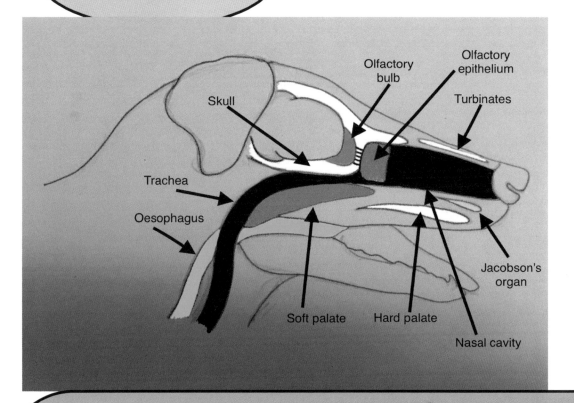

Part   **Function**

Nasal cavity   Open space behind the nose that allows air into the respiratory system

Olfactory epithelium   Located in the back of the nose it is a specialised network of epithelial cells and neurons. Neurons are stimulated by chemicals in the air and then send impulses to the olfactory bulb.

Olfactory bulb   Specialised region of the brain responsible for 'interpreting' smell.

Trachea   Also known as the windpipe it is a tube supported by rings of cartilage. Allows air to pass into the lungs.

Jacobson's organ   Specialised sensory organ seen in many mammal species. Highly sensitive to pheromones it allows animals to communicate with each other.

Turbinates   Network of bones inside the nasal cavity. Increases the surface area that air passes over as it enters the nose. Enables animals such as dogs to have an enhanced sense of smell.

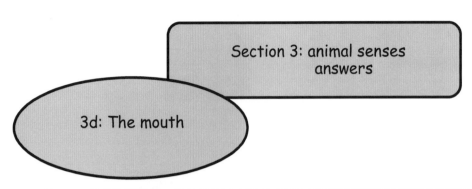

3d: The mouth

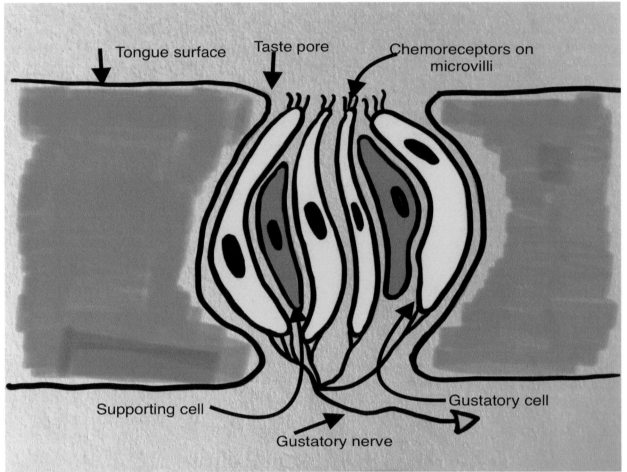

Part	Function
Taste pore	Opening on the surface of the tongue.
Chemoreceptors	Specialised receptors that detect chemicals in food & drink. Send an electrical impulse to the gustatory nerve.
Gustatory cell	Specialised cells containing chemoreceptors. Together with supporting cells makes up a 'taste bud'.
Gustatory nerve	Transmits the electrical impulse from the chemoreceptor to the brain.

Chemoreceptors on the tongue can detect 5 main tastes; sweet, salty, bitter, sour & umami.

Different flavours of foods are made up of different combinations of the 5 tastes.

3e: The skin

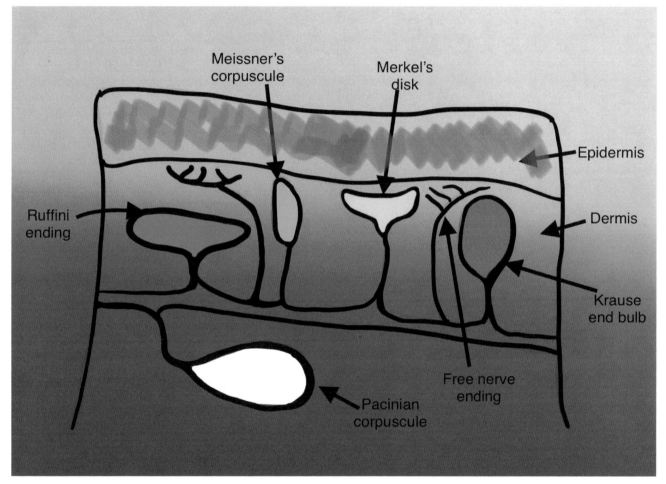

Part	Function
Meissner's corpuscle	Meissner's, Merkel's, Ruffini & Pacinian receptors all respond to texture, touch & pressure sensations. Some receptors such as Pacinian corpuscles are located deep within the dermis, other receptors are located much closer to the surface of the skin.
Merkel's disk	
Ruffini ending	
Pacinian corpuscle	
Krause end bulb	Responds to temperature change: usually a drop in temperature. Ruffini endings may also have a role in detecting increasing temperatures.

53

4a: Special adaptations

Name of adaptation	Description	Example of animals
Tapetum lucidum	Only works in animals that live in/near water. Specially adapted receptors known as Ampullae of Lorenzini, located around the nose & mouth can detect very weak electromagnetic fields that are produced by living organisms. This allows the animal to effectively find prey.	Horses, snakes, dogs, cats
1		2
	3	
Jacobson's organ	High frequency sound waves are emitted and the animal uses the echoes from nearby objects to determine direction, distance & speed in order to find prey, navigate & orientate themselves.	Dogs, cats, horses, deer
2		1
	4	
Electroreception	A specialised chemoreceptor found in many mammal species. Used to detect chemicals in the environment such as pheromones. Used by animals to communicate, often associated with readiness for reproduction. May also be used in determining aggressive tendencies & territorial disputes. Can also be used to detect prey.	Bats, toothed whales, dolphins
3		4
	2	
Echolocation	An extra layer at the back of the eye that sits behind the retina. It reflects additional light onto the retina which helps to improve vision, particularly at night. Seen in both predator & prey species, often either nocturnal or crepuscular animals.	Sharks & platypus
4		3
	1	

4b: Predator/prey
adaptations

Use this table to compare the sensory organs of predators & prey.

Predators	Prey
Eyes in front—binocular vision Good depth & speed perception	**Eyes** on the side—excellent peripheral vision, monocular vision.
Ears in front—funnel sound from in front, good for chasing down prey.	**Ears**—very mobile pinnae, very sensitive to quiet sounds.
Smell—highly developed, use of Jacobson's organ. Sharks have a very acute sense of smell under water, using their nostrils for detecting scent. Marine mammals, however, are believed to have a rather poor sense of smell.	**Smell**—use of Jacobson's organ, often highly sensitive.
Touch—animals such as fish use special sensory receptors that line each side of the body. Known as the lateral line, these receptors detect vibrations in the water and send impulses to the brain. Allows the animal to detect prey. Snakes are very sensitive to vibrations created by prey. Pads in paws also sensitive to vibrations.	**Touch**—may be sensitive to light touch, initiates flight response. Prey species will often move away from a source of pressure.
Taste—may rely more on smell than taste. Snakes use their tongue for smell rather than taste.	**Taste**—can be very sensitive, often more taste receptors in herbivores & omnivores than carnivores. Useful to detect poisonous plants in grazers & browsers. Rarely vomit.

55

Printed in Great Britain
by Amazon

27907749R00032